Bₚ Supplementary

Social Studies Program

How Series

HOW WE GET OUR MAIL

HOW DOCTORS HELP US

HOW HOSPITALS HELP US

HOW SCHOOLS HELP US

HOW WE CELEBRATE OUR SPRING HOLIDAYS

HOW FAMILIES LIVE TOGETHER

HOW WEATHER AFFECTS US

HOW AIRPLANES HELP US

HOW WE CELEBRATE OUR FALL HOLIDAYS

HOW WE GET OUR CLOTHING

HOW WE TRAVEL ON WATER

HOW FOODS ARE PRESERVED

HOW WE GET OUR DAIRY FOODS

HOW WE GET OUR CLOTH

HOW WE GET OUR SHELTER

HOW WE TRAVEL ON LAND

HOW PEOPLE LIVE IN THE BIG CITY

HOW COMMUNICATION HELPS US

HOW PRINTING HELPS US

Basic Concepts Series

HOW MAPS AND GLOBES HELP US

HOW CHARTS AND DRAWINGS HELP US

HOW PEOPLE LIVE IN AFRICA

HOW PEOPLE LIVE IN CANADA

HOW PEOPLE LIVE IN CENTRAL AMERICA

HOW PEOPLE LIVE IN JAPAN

HOW PEOPLE LIVE IN THE MIDDLE EAST

HOW THE NEW WORLD WAS DISCOVERED

HOW SCHOOLS AID DEMOCRACY

HOW DOCUMENTS PRESERVE FREEDOM

HOW OUR GOVERNMENT BEGAN

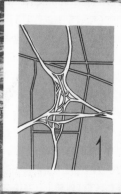

How Maps

and Globes Help Us

By **DAVID HACKLER**

Illustrated by **WILLIAM TANIS**

BENEFIC PRESS publishing division Beckley-Cardy Co.

CHICAGO Atlanta, Long Beach, Dallas, Portland

Maps and globes are tools which can help us in many ways. Maps help people travel by road, plane, and ship. They help us learn about our land, now and in the past. Maps and globes teach us much about far-away countries. Through them we become better acquainted with our world.

Contents

Library of Congress
Number 62-13998

The Earth

on Globes

How can we know the way our earth is shaped?

As we walk around on our earth, and look over it, the world seems to be flat. Even hills and mountains seem to rise from flat land.

But when we look at a photograph taken from one hundred miles above the earth, we can see how the earth is curved. We can see that we are looking at one side of something shaped like a ball.

What is the truest picture of the earth's surface?

Since the earth is shaped like a ball, the best picture of the earth is a globe. To see all of this picture of the earth, you will have to turn the globe. You cannot see more than one-half of the globe at once. The picture on this page shows only one-half of the globe.

What do we find on the surface of the earth?

On the surface of the globe, you see pictured both land and water. Since the globe is a kind of picture of our earth, this means that the surface of the earth is made up of land and water.

Some parts of the globe seem to show mostly water. Others picture large land areas. The land areas may be of many different colors, but the water areas are blue on your globe.

Is the earth mostly land or mostly water?

Your answer to this question may depend on the part of the globe you are looking at. It is possible to turn the globe so that you can see almost nothing but land. If you turn it another way, you will see almost nothing but water.

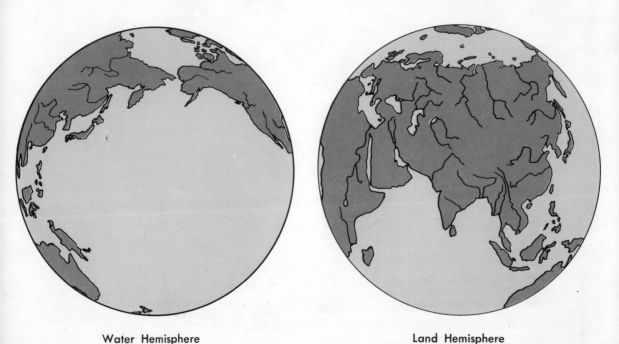

Water Hemisphere   Land Hemisphere

8

But if you turn the globe slowly so that you can see all the earth, you will find that the water areas are much greater than the land areas.

If we think of the whole surface of the earth as lying within a circle, the land and water areas would be divided like this:

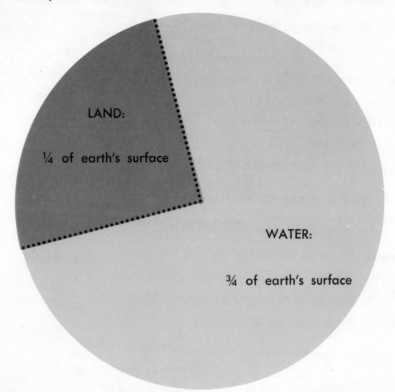

LAND:

¼ of earth's surface

WATER:

¾ of earth's surface

Why does the globe turn?

As you turn your globe, you may wonder why the globe is mounted so that it turns easily. For one thing, it is easier for you to see. But there is another reason.

The globe, turning on its stand, is much like the earth turning in space, so that first one side and then the other faces the sun. It turns completely around every twenty-four hours, causing the change on earth from day to night.

How are the earth and the globe different from a ball?

A ball usually has a smooth curved surface on which all parts are the same as all other parts. We do not say that a ball has a top or a bottom.

On the earth, and therefore on the globe, there is a point which we call the top of the earth. This is the <u>North Pole</u>, the point farthest north on the earth, or at the top of the globe.

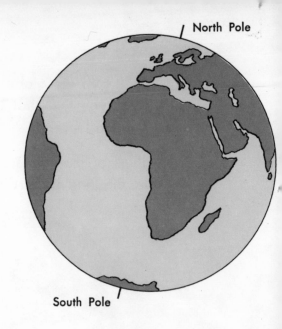

North Pole

South Pole

There is also a point at the bottom of the globe, the point farthest south, which is called the <u>South Pole</u>.

Of course there is nothing on the surface of the earth to show you where the poles are. If you should ever go to these two very cold spots, you would find nothing there but ice and snow.

What is the equator?

Halfway between the North Pole and the South Pole is a line drawn all the way around your globe. This line is called the <u>equator</u>. There is no line on the surface of the earth, of course. But this line on the globe helps us understand our earth.

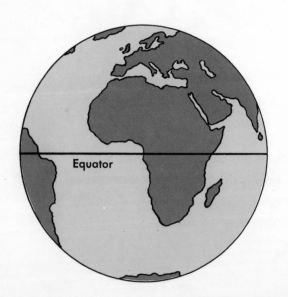

Equator

How can the earth be divided into two equal parts?

The shape of the earth and the globe has a special name. This shape is called a <u>sphere</u>. Half of a sphere is called a <u>hemisphere</u>.

Looking at the globe with the equator drawn on it, you can see that the earth can be divided into two equal parts. These are the Northern Hemisphere and the Southern Hemisphere.

Northern Hemisphere   Southern Hemisphere

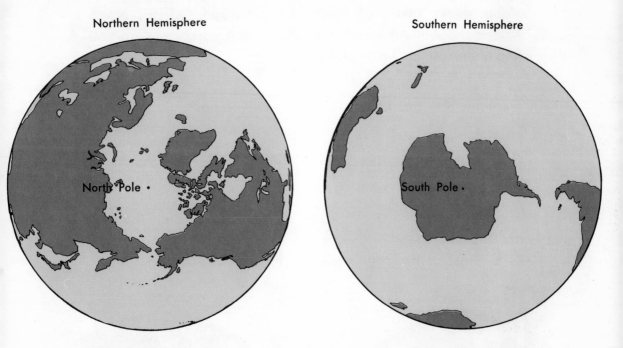

If we look at the globe from the top and then from the bottom, we can see the Northern, then the Southern Hemisphere.

Most of the areas near the equator are quite hot, just as the areas around the poles are very cold. This region near the equator is often called the <u>tropical region</u>. The area near the North Pole is called the <u>Arctic</u> region. Near the South Pole is the <u>Antarctic</u> region.

11

A line drawn around the globe through both of the poles can also divide the globe into two parts. A globe which has been divided in this way is shown at the bottom of this page. The two parts of this globe are called the Eastern Hemisphere and the Western Hemisphere.

What are the important land areas of the globe?

Large land areas of the globe are called <u>continents</u>. Your globe shows seven of them: Asia, Europe, Africa, North America, South America, Australia and Antarctica. Can you find them all on your globe?

What are the names of the four great oceans?

Find on your globe the largest water areas: the Atlantic Ocean, the Pacific Ocean, the Indian Ocean, and the Arctic Ocean.

You will see that the continents of North and South America are the main land areas in the Western Hemisphere. Most of the rest of the continents are in the Eastern Hemisphere.

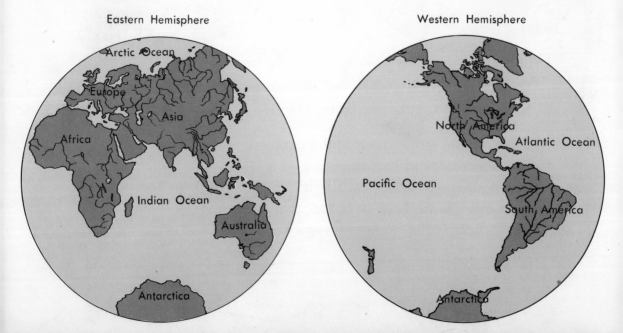

Eastern Hemisphere

Western Hemisphere

How We Use Globes

The globe can help us find many of the places in which we are interested. We can find the <u>position</u> of such a place, its exact location.

Usually, before we try to find the exact location of a place, we know on which continent to look. If it is a very large place, a good-sized country, it is not hard to find the place we are looking for just by hunting around on the right part of the globe.

But there is a special method for finding an exact location on the globe.

North Pole

South Pole

How is position shown on a globe?

Lines are drawn on the globe to help us find the position of the place we are looking for.

The lines running from top to bottom, from the North Pole to the South Pole, are called lines of <u>longitude</u>.

The lines which run across the globe, in the same way that the equator runs, are called lines of <u>latitude</u>.

You can find any place on the earth if you know on which lines of latitude and longitude it is.

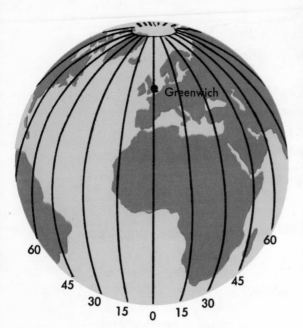

How are lines of longitude drawn and numbered?

Lines of longitude divide the globe into sections like sections of an orange. These lines meet at the North Pole and at the South Pole. They divide the globe into 360 sections all the same size.

Longitude lines are numbered in degrees. <u>Degrees</u> are parts of a complete circle.

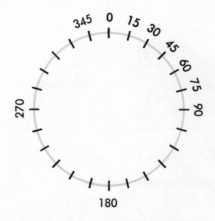

Globe makers from different countries agreed to start numbering the longitude lines at the line which runs through <u>Greenwich, England</u>. Beginning at Greenwich, lines of longitude are numbered from 0 to 180 degrees west, and from 0 to 180 degrees east. There is only one line on the globe numbered 180 degrees, and that is exactly opposite the line running through Greenwich.

Longitude lines are sometimes called <u>meridians</u>. Not all of them can be shown on a globe. On this globe only one in each fifteen longitude lines is shown.

14

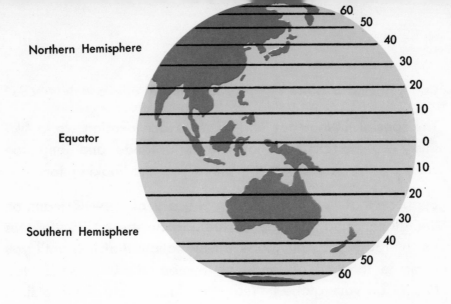

Northern Hemisphere

Equator

Southern Hemisphere

60
50
40
30
20
10
0
10
20
30
40
50
60

How are lines of latitude drawn and numbered?

Lines of latitude cross the lines of longitude much as streets cross in a town. The equator is the line of latitude that is halfway between the North Pole and the South Pole. It is numbered 0 on the map.

Beginning at the equator, lines of latitude are numbered from 0 to 90 degrees north latitude and from 0 to 90 degrees south latitude. Lines of latitude do not meet. They are sometimes called parallels.

When you look at the globe from one side, with the equator in the middle, it will look like the picture at the top of the page. You will not be able to see the latitude lines at the very top and bottom of the globe. They seem to disappear over the top and under the bottom of the globe's curved surface.

That is why the picture does not show lines numbered 70 and 80. Even if you look at the very top of a real globe, you will not see a line numbered 90. It would be right where the North Pole is.

Can you find a place if you know its latitude and longitude?

The special method for finding an exact location works like this. You must know what lines of latitude and longitude cross at the location of the place you are looking for.

Suppose that you want to find the city of New Orleans on the globe. Find the line of latitude numbered 30 degrees north. (30 N on your globe.) Now follow that line until you come to the line of longitude numbered 90 degrees west (90 W on your globe.) Near the place where the two lines cross you will find New Orleans.

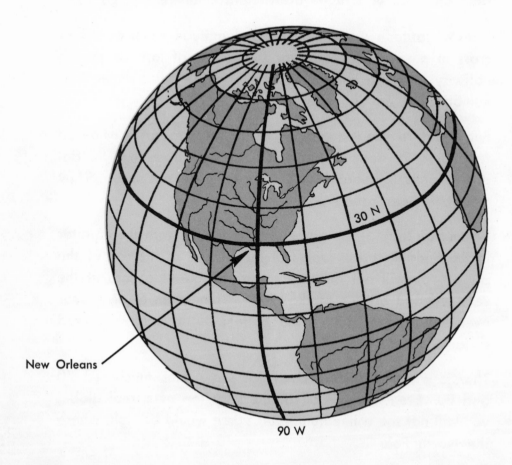

New Orleans

30 N

90 W

Why are globes useful?

A globe is an almost exact picture of the surface of the earth. Since the earth's surface is curved, it cannot be shown on a flat surface unless it is changed. But the globe shows the picture of the earth on a curved surface like the earth itself.

Your globe can show true directions and distances between different parts of the world. All land and water areas are shown in their true sizes and shapes. Studying a globe is the best way to find out what the earth looks like.

Why We Use Maps

A <u>map</u> is a drawing of part of the earth on a flat surface. It looks something like the earth would look if you were flying a mile or two above it in a plane.

The map does not show everything that a photograph shows. It shows only those things that are important to the people using the map.

It can show many things that a globe cannot show. The globe is a picture of the whole earth and does not have room for much detail. The map can show a small part or a large part of the earth's surface.

This map shows roads, buildings, trees, and a river.

Other maps may show other features.

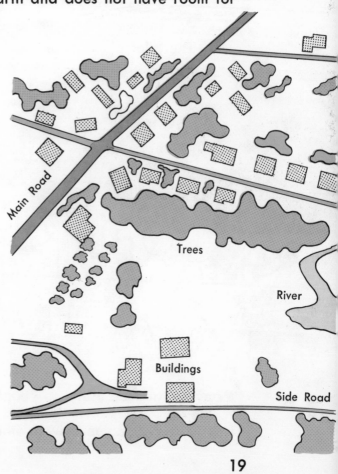

19

Aerial Photograph Co., Chicago

How do maps help travelers?

Travelers need maps to find their way from one place to another. A family on a long automobile trip would not know which way to go without a map.

The pilot of a plane needs a special map to guide him in approaching the airport.

Maps can also be useful to people who are traveling on foot.

It is hard to imagine travel without maps.

How do maps help students?

Maps have another very important purpose. They tell us useful facts about our country and other parts of the world. Maps show us where towns, mountains, and rivers are.

A map can be made to show how much rain falls each year in the various parts of a country. Another might show what kinds of trees grow in different regions.

From maps students can learn the chief crops and the important products of the country they are studying.

Position on a Map

Maps tell us where to find any place on earth. They tell us the position of the place, its exact location.

How can you find your position on the map of a city?

Look at this map showing part of an imaginary city. The streets form a criss-cross pattern.

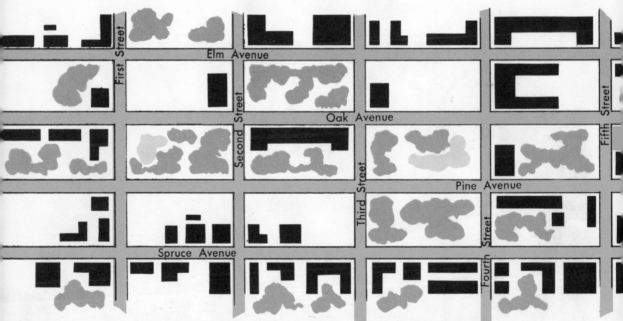

On the map of the city, find the line which stands for Third Street. Keep your finger on that line while you look for Elm Avenue. To find the corner of the two streets, find the place where these two lines cross.

How do we find position on a large map?

The map of the United States also has regularly spaced lines, running from top to bottom of the map, and from side to side. These are the lines of longitude and the lines of latitude which are also found on your globe. They have the same purpose on the map as on the globe—to help us find the position of places. These lines have numbers, so that you can tell one from another, just as you tell streets apart by their names.

Six cities are marked by dots on this map. Can you find the city of Denver, Colorado? Here are clues to help you. Look for a line running from the top of the map to the bottom, which has the number 105. Now find a line running across the map, which has the number 40. Where do these lines meet? Very close to that spot you will find Denver.

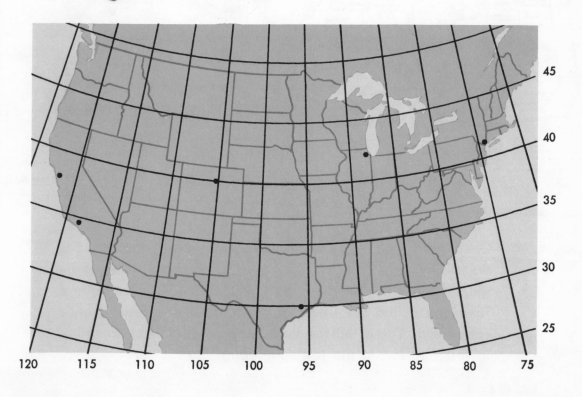

How does a road map show position?

On a road map, the lines running from top to bottom and across the map are not numbered in degrees. The north-south lines have numbers and the east-west lines letters. Towns and cities are listed with a number and letter beside each town. These tell the map reader which lines to follow in order to locate the town he wants.

Direction on a Map

Maps tell us which way to go to get from one place to another. They tell us <u>direction</u>.

It is easy to walk across the street to a neighbor's house. You need only look at the house and start walking in that direction.

It is not so easy for people who travel long distances to places they cannot see. These people must find the direction to travel from a map.

How do lines of longitude show direction?

One way to tell direction from the map is by means of the lines of longitude. You remember that all lines of longitude run north and south. On many maps these lines run from top to bottom. They show that north is at the top and south at the bottom of the map. East is on the right side of the map, while west is on the left.

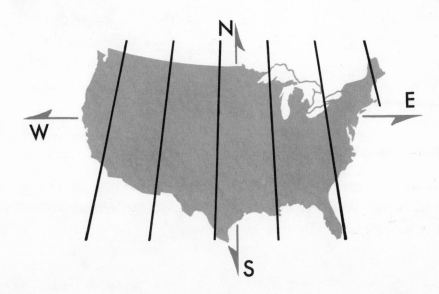

Can a map compass help find directions?

Another way to tell direction is to look for the compass which is drawn on many maps. The <u>map compass</u> is a drawing showing directions.

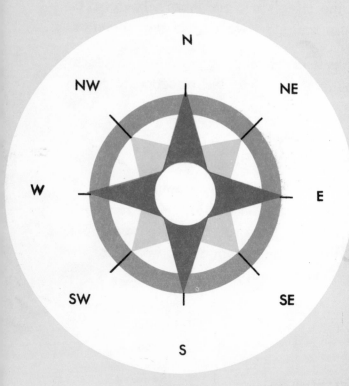

North is always marked on this drawing. It points to the direction which is north on the map. Often, but not always, this is the top of the map.

When north is at the top, south is at the bottom, east to the right, and west to the left.

The four other directions shown on the compass are northeast (NE), southeast (SE), southwest (SW), and northwest (NW).

How can we find our directions on the earth's surface?

There are several ways to find directions on the earth's surface when you are traveling from place to place. You can use a compass, the sun, or the stars.

How do we use the magnetic compass?

A compass has a magnetic needle which always points toward a place near the North Pole called magnetic north. <u>Magnetic north</u> is a point on the earth, near the North Pole, which attracts the compass needle.

The compass which you use in traveling is mounted over a card much like the drawing on page 26.

To find the direction you are traveling, twist the compass in your hand until the needle points to N. Then you can read your direction of travel from the outside edge of the compass.

This boy is facing northwest.

Can the sun or stars help us find direction?

You need to know the time of day to find your directions from the sun.

At 12:00 o'clock noon, your shadow will point just about north. If you face your shadow, your right hand points toward east, and your left hand points toward west. South is behind you.

During Daylight Saving Time, your shadow will point north at 1:00 P.M.

There is another way that you can get a good idea of directions, if you don't have a compass to find them more exactly. You know that the sun rises in the east and sets in the west. This will help you find east in the early morning, or west in the late afternoon.

North Star

At night, you may be able to find north using the North Star. Although this star is not one of the brightest, you can find it by knowing where to look.

First you must find the Big Dipper. It has four stars which make up the cup and three which make the handle. The two stars of the cup that are farthest from the handle point to the North Star. The direction of north is on the earth just beneath the North Star.

Distance on a Map

You can find the distance between any two places on the map if you know how to use the map scale. The <u>map scale</u> relates the distance between two points on the map to the distance between the same two points on the surface of the earth.

The map scale is usually at the bottom or the corner of the map. It is a line marked off in some unit of distance—in miles, yards, or feet. The map scale tells you how much distance on the map stands for how much distance on earth.

Why do we need many different scales?

You may wonder why there are so many different scales. In a book of maps where the pages are all the same size, each map is a picture of a different part of the earth's surface. Some maps, therefore, show larger areas than others.

Here is the map of a schoolyard. The scale shows that an inch on the map is equal to 100 feet on the earth's surface.

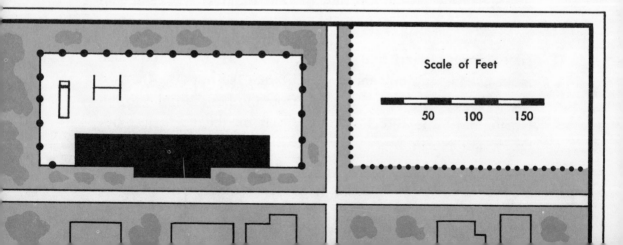

Scale of Feet

50 100 150

LAKE

MICHIGAN

This map scale
shows that an
inch on the map
is equal to seven
miles on the earth's
surface.

CHICAGO

Scale of Miles

1 3 5 7

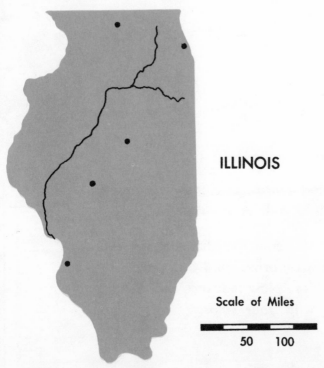

ILLINOIS

This scale shows
that an inch on
the map equals
one hundred miles
on the surface of
the earth.

Scale of Miles

50   100

31

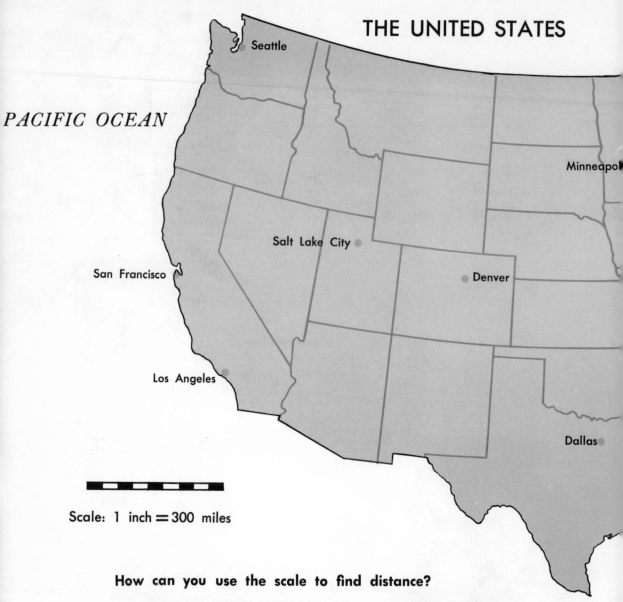

THE UNITED STATES

PACIFIC OCEAN

Seattle

Minneapo[l]

Salt Lake City

Denver

San Francisco

Los Angeles

Dallas

Scale: 1 inch = 300 miles

How can you use the scale to find distance?

On this map of the United States, one inch is equal to 300 miles. Check this scale with your ruler.

Suppose that you want to know the distance between two cities: San Francisco, California, and Salt Lake City, Utah. First locate both cities. Now measure the distance between them carefully with your ruler.

Buffalo

Detroit

Chicago

Philadelphia

New York City

Washington, D.C.

is

Atlanta

New Orleans

ATLANTIC OCEAN

The distance is about two inches. If an inch stands for 300 miles, two inches must represent 600 miles. You know, then, that the distance between the two cities is just about 600 miles.

How does the mileage table give us exact distances?

Using a map scale and a ruler usually does not give us the exact distance between two cities. We have another way of finding exact distances between cities. That is the mileage table, a listing of cities showing the distance between any two of them. The mileage table for the map on pages 32 and 33 lists only those cities shown on that map. These are listed alphabetically down the left side and again across the top of the table.

In the table on page 35, find San Francisco in the left-hand column. Hold one finger there. Then find Salt Lake City in the row across the top. Run one finger across the row from San Francisco and another down the column from Salt Lake City. In the box where the row and column meet is the number which tells you how many miles there are between the two cities.

Try finding the distance between New York City and Buffalo, New York. First measure the length of the line between them on the map, and compare it with the scale. "Just about an inch," you will say, or "300 miles."

Now look up the distance in the mileage table. Here you will find that the exact distance is 292 miles. The distances on the table are airline distances, the length in miles of the shortest air route between two cities.

Choose two other cities, in different states, and find how far apart they are. Use the ruler and map scale first, then look up the distance on the table.

Airline Distances Between Cities

	Atlanta	Buffalo	Chicago	Dallas	Denver	Detroit	Los Angeles	Minneapolis	New Orleans	New York City	Philadelphia	Salt Lake City	San Francisco	Seattle	Washington, D. C.
Atlanta, Ga.		697	587	721	1212	596	1936	907	424	748	666	1583	2139	2182	543
Buffalo, N. Y.	697		454	1198	1370	216	2198	731	1086	292	279	1699	2300	2117	292
Chicago, Ill.	587	454		803	920	238	1745	355	833	713	666	1260	1858	1737	597
Dallas, Tex.	721	1198	803		663	999	1240	862	443	1374	1299	999	1483	1681	1185
Denver, Colo.	1212	1370	920	663		1156	831	700	1082	1631	1579	371	949	1021	1494
Detroit, Mich.	596	216	238	999	1156		1983	543	939	482	443	1492	2091	1938	396
Los Angeles, Calif.	1936	2198	1745	1240	831	1983		1524	1673	2451	2394	579	347	959	2300
Minneapolis, Minn.	907	731	355	862	700	543	1524		1051	1018	985	987	1584	1395	934
New Orleans, La.	424	1086	833	443	1082	939	1673	1051		1171	1089	1434	1926	2101	966
New York, N. Y.	748	292	713	1374	1631	482	2451	1018	1171		83	1972	2571	2408	205
Philadelphia, Pa.	666	279	666	1299	1579	443	2394	985	1089	83		1925	2523	2380	123
Salt Lake City, Utah	1583	1699	1260	999	371	1492	579	987	1434	1972	1925		600	701	1848
San Francisco, Calif.	2139	2300	1858	1483	949	2091	347	1584	1926	2571	2523	600		678	2442
Seattle, Wash.	2182	2117	1737	1681	1021	1938	959	1395	2101	2408	2380	701	678		2329
Washington, D. C.	543	292	597	1185	1494	396	2300	934	966	205	123	1848	2442	2329	

How Maps Are Made

Most maps are drawings of part of the earth's surface. Sometimes, however, we need a drawing of the whole earth, on a flat surface.

A globe gives the best picture of the earth, because it has the same shape as the earth itself. Yet we often need a larger picture of the earth's surface than can be put on the globe. One which hangs on the wall is easier to study and shows the whole world at the same time. We also need smaller maps which can be printed in books.

What is the map maker's problem?

The map maker must show the outside surface of the round globe on a flat map.

If you try to flatten out an orange peel, the peel will stretch and lose its shape. It will look a little like this:

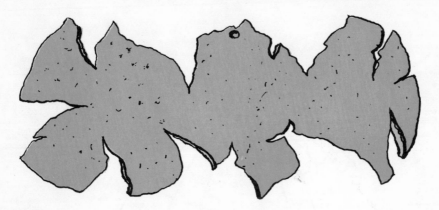

This is the map maker's problem. No matter how hard he tries, he cannot make a true likeness of the round earth on a flat sheet of paper. He has to stretch his map or cut it a little, just as you would have to stretch or cut an orange peel to make it lie flat.

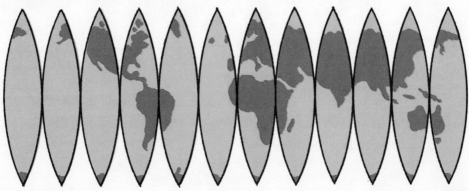

How has this problem been solved?

The map maker has found a way to solve his problem.

Suppose that the world is drawn on a glass globe. The drawing on the globe is curved, just as the surface of the earth is curved.

If a light is placed inside the globe, the shadows of the land and water surfaces drawn on the globe will fall on a screen hung nearby.

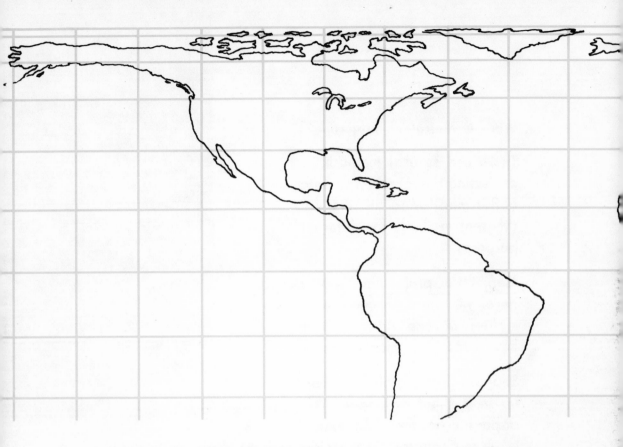

This is the screen on which the shadows of the Western Hemisphere have fallen.

This is called a map projection. The map maker uses a pro-jection to show the round earth on a flat sheet of paper.

This shadow projection, if left just as it is, would make a very poor map. At the top of this projection, the parallels are so close together that this map would be useless. At the same time, the meridians, which on the globe meet at the North Pole, are spread apart. The North Pole, which is really a point, becomes a line.

The mapmaker has to change this projection to make a map we can use.

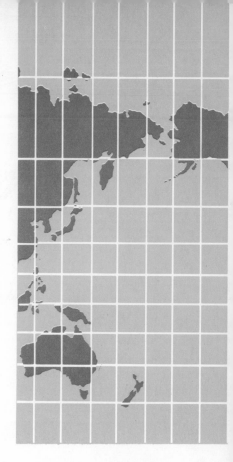

What is Mercator's projection?

There are several methods of projecting the round earth onto a flat map. Map makers use different methods for different purposes.

Mercator's projection, shown here, was used by most map makers at one time. This is how a Mercator map is made.

Suppose that a globe is rolled up in a sheet of paper. The paper touches the globe exactly on the equator. The projection light is placed in the center of the globe.

The light throws shadows of the earth's surface on the rolled sheet of paper. At the equator, the shadows are the same size as the areas on the globe.

But near the poles, the shadows are much larger than the areas on the globe. The top of the world has to be very much stretched in both directions before it can be pictured on a flat map.

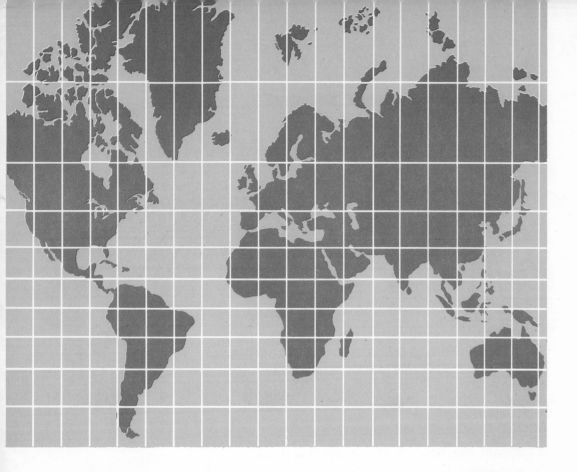

Mercator's projection is often used to make maps for seamen. Mercator maps are good for ocean travel, because they make it easy to find directions and distances for long ocean trips.

How does a Mercator map show shape and size?

The advantage of a Mercator map is that areas of the world have the same shape on the map that they do on earth. However, the student cannot get a true idea of the size of certain areas. The map maker has drawn the areas near the North and South Pole very large in proportion to the areas near the equator. He has done this to show them in their correct position of longitude and latitude.

What is an interrupted projection?

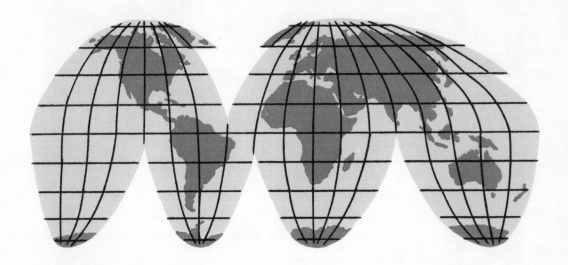

This map is called an <u>interrupted projection</u> because it stops and starts again. It was made by cutting the picture of the earth's surface in the middle of the oceans, and then flattening it out.

It is often used in geography books and books of maps. It is helpful in learning about different parts of the world, because it shows land areas as they are really shaped. At the same time, it does not give a false idea about their size.

The map maker in this case does not try to show the shape and size of the oceans. He has not made this map for people who want to travel. He has made it for people who want to study land areas.

How do these two projections compare?

No matter how the round earth is pictured on a flat surface, something has to be changed. In the Mercator projection, directions and shapes of areas are correct.

But land areas appear out of proportion as they get farther away from the equator.

Compare the two pictures of Greenland, an island which is just east of North America in the North Atlantic Ocean. The Mercator map makes Greenland appear to be larger than South America.

Greenland As It Appears on the Globe

Greenland As It Appears on Mercator's Projection

The Atlantic Ocean

In the interrupted projection the shapes and sizes of land areas are almost the same as on the globe.

But the directions and distances between land areas are not shown correctly. Lines of longitude which run through the ocean are interrupted and sometimes lost. A sailor could not find his course from this map.

How is an equal area map made?

When the map maker is drawing only part of the earth's surface, his map can be more nearly correct. Only a part of the earth's curved surface has to be drawn on the flat map.

There are many ways of doing this. Here is one, called the equal area map.

The map maker has laid out longitude and latitude lines like streets in a city. Within each four-sided section, he has pictured an area of the earth's surface. The area pictured in any section is equal to the area pictured in any other section.

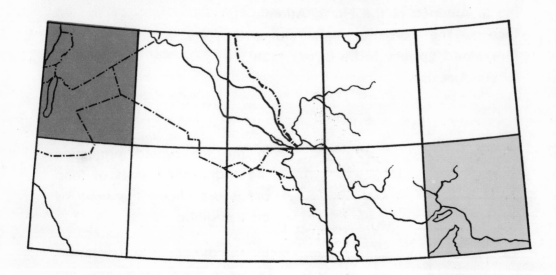

The area colored red on the map is the same size as the area colored blue. They both stand for the same number of square miles on the earth's surface. Within both areas a square inch on the map stands for 80,656 square miles on the surface of the earth.

The artist makes many small changes in shape and direction in order to show the curved surface of the earth on a flat map.

Why are several kinds of projections in use?

Maps are made for different uses. The map maker decides what changes to make in the picture of the earth's surface by thinking about how the map is to be used.

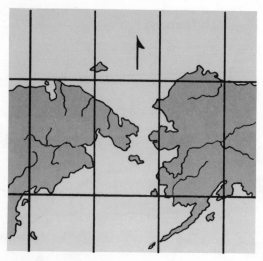

Travelers need a map which shows directions correctly. This is more important to them than being able to compare the size of one country with that of another. The explorers and sea captains of long ago wanted maps on which directions agreed with compass directions.

Students who are studying other parts of the world do not need to have all of the oceans' area on the map they use. They would rather have a map which shows the shape and size of the country they are studying.

Colors and Symbols

Color is used on maps to tell us important things about the earth's surface. We can find rivers, forests, hills, and valleys on the map because of the way they are colored.

On most maps a certain color will always stand for a certain kind of thing.

How is color used to show physical features?

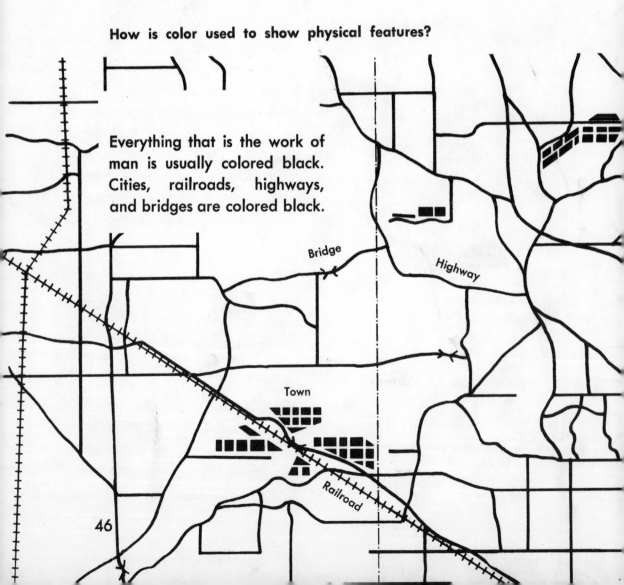

Everything that is the work of man is usually colored black. Cities, railroads, highways, and bridges are colored black.

Bridge

Highway

Town

Railroad

46

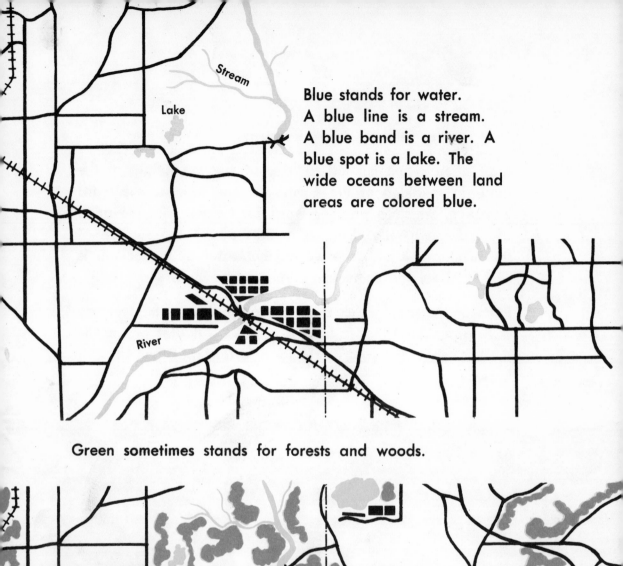

Blue stands for water.
A blue line is a stream.
A blue band is a river. A
blue spot is a lake. The
wide oceans between land
areas are colored blue.

Green sometimes stands for forests and woods.

How is color used to show elevation?

Most often green is used to help us see the height of the land. In speaking of the earth's surface, we use the word elevation, which is another word for height. The elevation of land means the distance it rises above the surface of the oceans. All over the world, the water of the oceans is at just about the same level. This is known as sea level.

Parts of the map which show the earth near sea level are dark green, and higher land is colored a lighter green. As the land rises, the color is changed to tan, and then to dark brown.

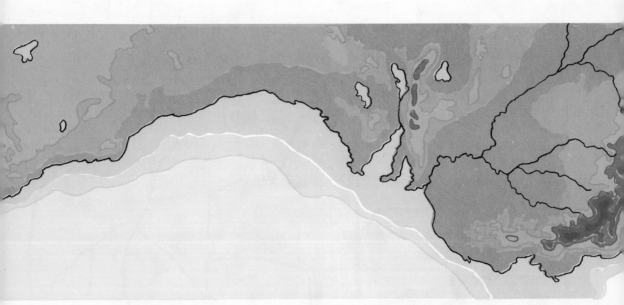

Different shades of blue stand for different depths of water in the oceans. On this map the lighter shades stand for deeper water.

How may colors show different countries?

On this page is a map of the continent of Europe. Continent is the name given to one of the seven large land areas of the earth. The continent of Europe is divided into many countries.

These countries are shown in several different colors. Here they are used to help you see where the area of one country ends, and that of another begins.

Boundaries, or limits of area of countries, are clearer because of the different colors used for different countries. The size and shape of each country stand out through the use of color.

49

What is a map symbol?

Map symbols are another way the map maker gives us information. A map <u>symbol</u> is a drawing which stands for something real on the earth's surface.

Here is a photograph of part of a small town.

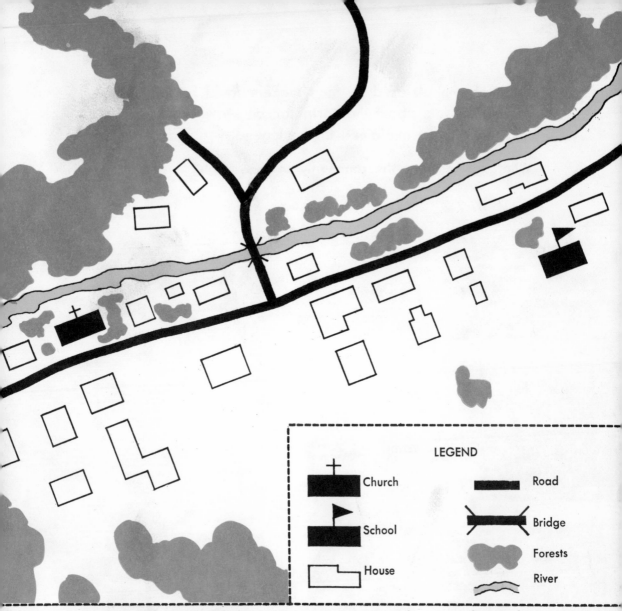

LEGEND

✝ Church

🚩 School

🏠 House

▬ Road

✕ Bridge

Forests

〜 River

This map pictures the same area as the photograph on the opposite page. Important features, such as the church, the school, and the river are shown by symbols.

The symbols used on this map are explained in a key called the <u>legend</u> which you can find in a corner of the map.

Some map symbols are used on many different maps—the symbol for a road, for instance.

A list of symbols used by map makers could be very long. Almost any fact about the earth can be shown on a map, if the symbols are explained in the legend.

What are some of the commonly used symbols?

Desert

Swamp

Forest

Unimproved Road

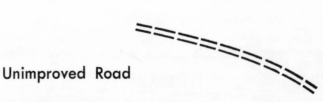

Highway

Railroad

Airport

Bridge

Church  53

How is the shape of the earth's surface shown?

Hills and valleys, mountains and rolling plains are shown on maps by lines called <u>contour lines</u>. Contour means shape, and these lines show the natural shape of the earth's surface.

Every point along one of these lines is the same number of feet above sea level.

Contour lines tell us much about the earth's surface. If they are far apart, the land is almost flat or gently sloping.

Gently
Rolling
Land

United Press International

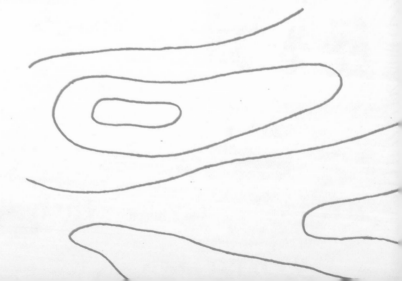

Contour lines close together tell us that the land is steep and hilly.

The tops of hills are shown by the shortest lines. A number at the top of a hill tells how many feet above sea level the hill rises.

Steeply
Rising
Land

United Press International

7632

What can be shown on a small area map?

Maps of small areas can show very fine details. They show each farm and factory, bridge and stream. They show all the railroads, churches, and schools.

These maps show each street in even the smallest towns.

Because they show such fine detail, small area maps can show only a small part of the earth's surface.

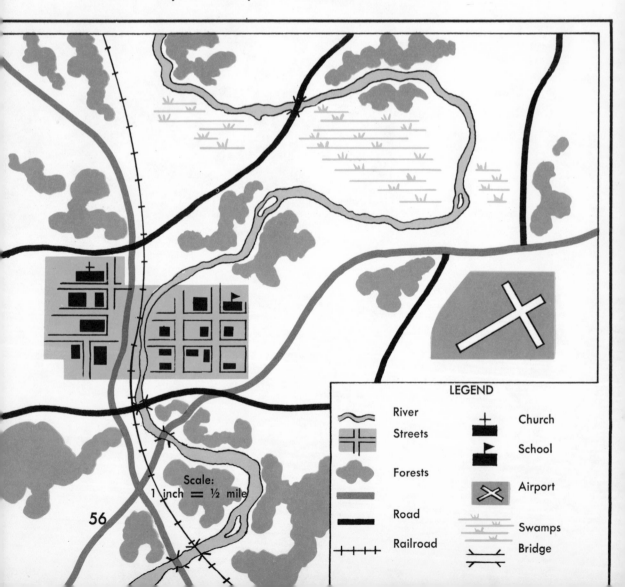

Scale:
1 inch = ½ mile

56

LEGEND

River	Church
Streets	School
Forests	Airport
Road	Swamps
Railroad	Bridge

What can be shown on a large area map?

Maps of large areas show only the larger cities and rivers. Often they do not show any highways or railroads.

Large area maps can show whole countries at one time. On these maps the students can see the shape of sea coasts and mountain ranges. They can see the boundaries of countries.

Because they show so large a part of the world, they cannot show the small towns and little streams that small area maps can show.

NORTH AMERICA

Scale:
1 inch = 1040 miles

How are symbols used on an air map?

This map is like those used by airplane pilots. It tells them many special things they must know in order to fly their airplanes safely.

It tells them where to find the airports. It tells them which radio stations to use when they are flying at night or in bad weather.

The contour lines show the shape of the earth's surface. These lines are very important if the pilot is flying near mountains. The pilot needs to know where the mountain peaks are, so that he won't fly into them.

Other features, such as cities, rivers, roads, and railroads, are marked so that the pilot can check his position by landmarks. A <u>vertical obstruction,</u> which you will find in the legend, is anything high which the pilot might hit.

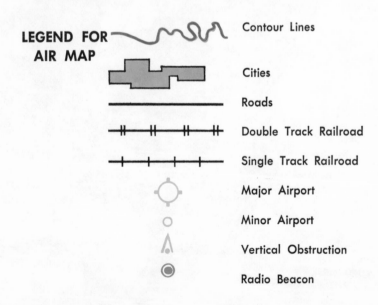

LEGEND FOR AIR MAP

Contour Lines

Cities

Roads

Double Track Railroad

Single Track Railroad

Major Airport

Minor Airport

Vertical Obstruction

Radio Beacon

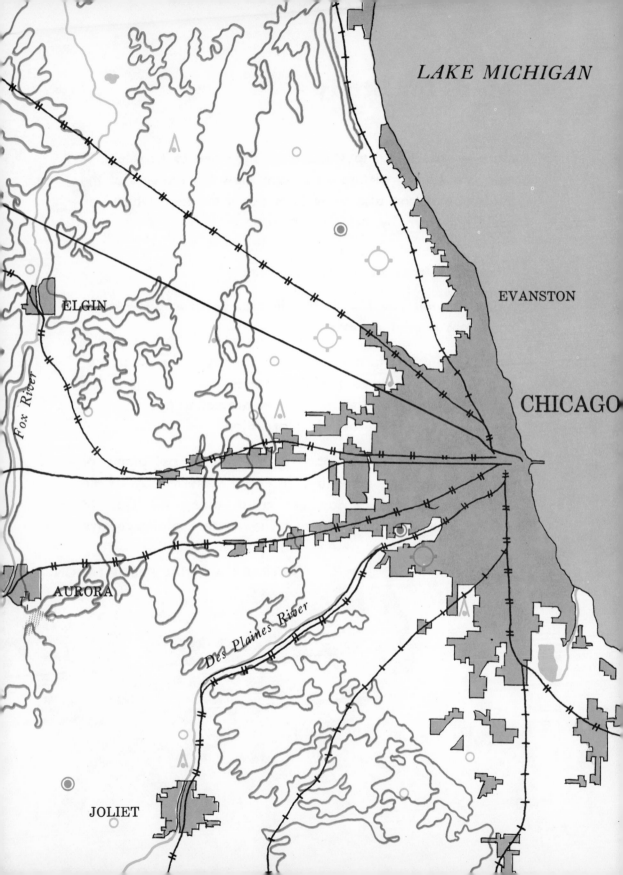

LAKE MICHIGAN

EVANSTON

CHICAGO

ELGIN

Fox River

AURORA

Des Plaines River

JOLIET

Maps for Study

Maps are as useful to students as they are to travelers. A map is a kind of picture which can show the features of the landscape. It can also show facts about the land which you could not learn by traveling through it.

What can a map show us about climate?

Maps can tell you about the <u>climate</u>, or average weather conditions over a number of years.

An important fact to know about a country is the amount of rain that falls each year in different sections. This is called the <u>rainfall</u>. Rain and snow together are called <u>precipitation.</u> The map below pictures this information.

The legend shows which parts of the country get plenty of rain and which are quite dry. The northwestern coast of the United States and its southern coast, along the Gulf of Mexico, receive plenty of rain. The western plains receive very little.

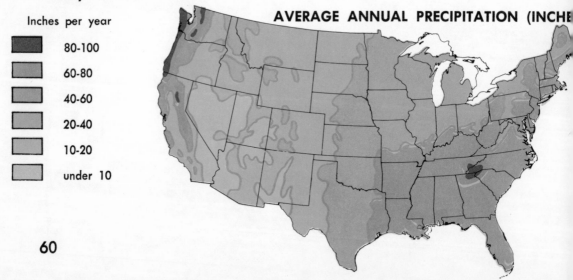

Inches per year

80-100
60-80
40-60
20-40
10-20
under 10

AVERAGE ANNUAL PRECIPITATION (INCHE

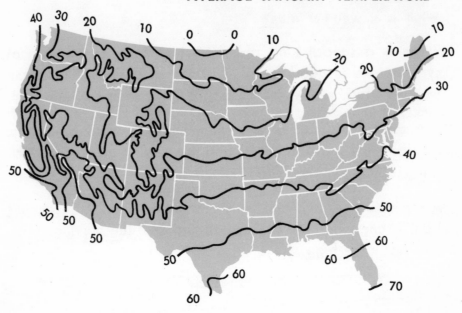

AVERAGE JANUARY TEMPERATURE

A symbol called an isotherm is used in this map. An <u>isotherm</u> is a line joining certain points on the map. Each of these points stands for a place having the same temperature at a certain time. On this map, the isotherms show the average temperature in January in different parts of the United States.

As you would expect, the coldest January temperatures are to be found in the northern part of the country. But this map can show you something else which influences temperature in different places.

Follow with your eyes the northern border of the United States, from the Pacific Ocean to the middle of the continent. Notice how the numbers standing for January temperatures get smaller as you go inland. You have discovered an important fact about climate. Land areas farther from the ocean almost always have colder winter temperatures than the areas closer to the ocean on the same line of latitude. Oceans, therefore, have an influence on climate.

What is a weather map?

There is a special kind of map which uses its own set of symbols and is good for only a day at a time. This is the weather map, which you have probably seen on television.

It is an outline map of a region, showing wind directions, high and low pressure areas, and the moving air fronts which bring about weather changes.

A <u>stationary front</u> is one which is not moving. An <u>occluded front</u> is one with cold air on both sides of the moving front, and warm air high above it.

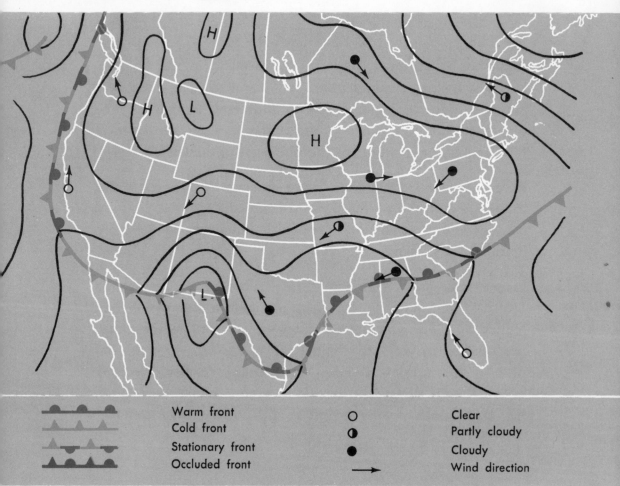

Warm front
Cold front
Stationary front
Occluded front

○ Clear
◐ Partly cloudy
● Cloudy
→ Wind direction

Center of high and low pressure areas shown by H and L

The next day the area outline will be the same, but the symbols and markings on the map will be in different places to show how the weather is changing.

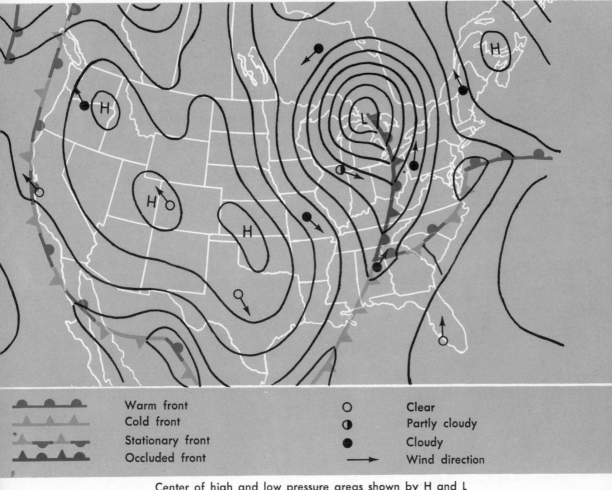

Warm front	○	Clear
Cold front	◐	Partly cloudy
Stationary front	●	Cloudy
Occluded front	→	Wind direction

Center of high and low pressure areas shown by H and L

People can understand the weather report much more easily when they can see it on a map. In the newspaper, weather information can be given in less space by using a map than by writing a story.

Can a map show how mountains influence rainfall?

It is interesting to put together what we have learned from different maps. Often, we can learn something new this way.

On the physical map of the United States, page 57, find the mountainous areas of the West. Next find these same areas on the rainfall map, page 60. You will notice that west of the western mountains, on the Pacific coast, the rainfall is quite heavy. Just east of them and on their eastern slopes are the driest parts of the country. We see that rain clouds formed over the Pacific Ocean cannot cross the high mountains to bring rain to the Great Plains.

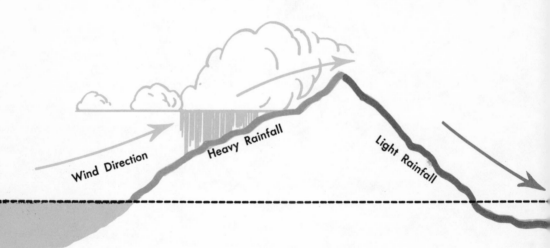

Wind Direction   Heavy Rainfall   Light Rainfall

This is a fact about the climate of our country which we see and understand through studying maps. In the same way, by studying the map on page 61, you learned that oceans make the climate of nearby land areas warmer in winter.

Maps teach us facts about our country. Even more important, they show us the reasons which explain the facts.

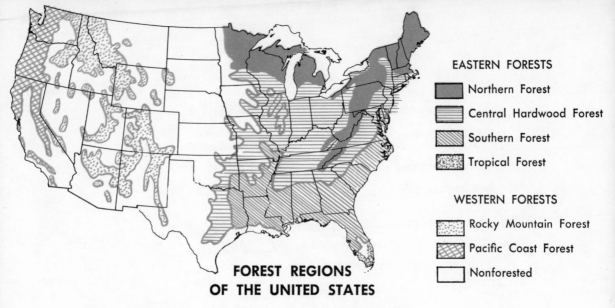

**FOREST REGIONS
OF THE UNITED STATES**

Can a map show how rainfall affects forests?

Look carefully at the title and legend of this map. The part of the map colored green stands for land on which forests grew before it was cleared for farms and cities.

If you live in the eastern part of the country or on the Pacific coast, trees probably line the streets of your town. Many kinds of trees grow in yards, even though most of the trees which grew there long ago have been cut down.

The white part of the map stands for the area of our country where trees will not grow naturally, without special care. Here towns and farms may have a few trees, but someone had to plant them and take care of them.

There are reasons why few trees grow on the prairies and plains. The map on page 60 shows one reason. This map shows that the prairies and plains have very light rainfall. Trees grow best where there is plenty of rain.

Here is a relationship between two facts, one about rainfall and the other about forest growth. You can see the relationship because the facts have been pictured on maps.

Do maps sometimes show how land is used?

The maps we have studied so far in this chapter have pictured natural facts. Man has had no influence over rainfall or temperature.

But man has changed the land by the way he has used it. Maps can show the different ways people have used the land of our country. Here is a map showing the amount of land used for raising crops.

TOTAL CROPLAND 1954

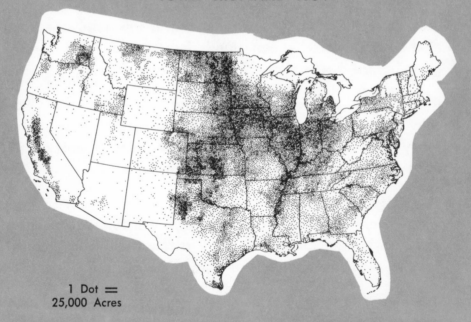

1 Dot =
25,000 Acres

The legend tells us the <u>acreage</u> (or number of acres) that each dot stands for. The parts of the map which are most nearly black represent the best farming land in the country.

Look again at the map on page 60. You will see that more farming is done on land which gets plenty of rain.

66

The study of maps can take us one step farther in our understanding of how man uses land.

This map shows the areas where cotton is grown in the United States.

You can see at once that cotton needs a warm climate. It is grown only in the southern part of the country.

COTTON HARVEST 1954

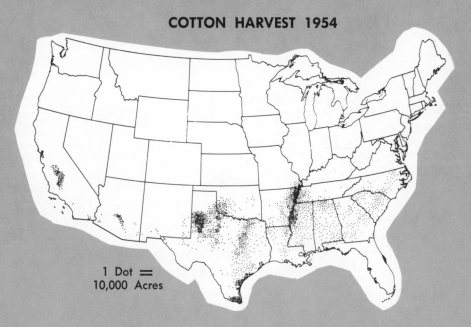

1 Dot =
10,000 Acres

Looking at this map and the rainfall map tells you something else: cotton needs a climate which is not too damp. Little cotton is raised close to the Gulf of Mexico or Atlantic Ocean.

Maps are made to show many other important uses of the land. This kind of map is usually made by men who work for departments of our government. Farmers and business men need this information in their work.

Can maps show where people live and why?

The eastern part of the United States has a dense <u>population</u>, which means that large numbers of people live there.

Since so many people live there, we might guess that people from Europe settled first in the eastern part of our country. And we would be right. We could also guess that the eastern part of our country has a good climate. We could guess that it is easy to grow crops there. A look at the rainfall map would show that we were right.

A <u>metropolitan area</u> is a large city with its suburbs. Let us look at the largest metropolitan area in the country. The arrow points to the New York metropolitan area.

Why does the New York area have so many people?

New York has the finest harbor on the east coast. West of New York is a valley which is the best route to the Middle West. At New York some of the most important trade routes of the world come together. This makes it a good place for many people to earn a living.

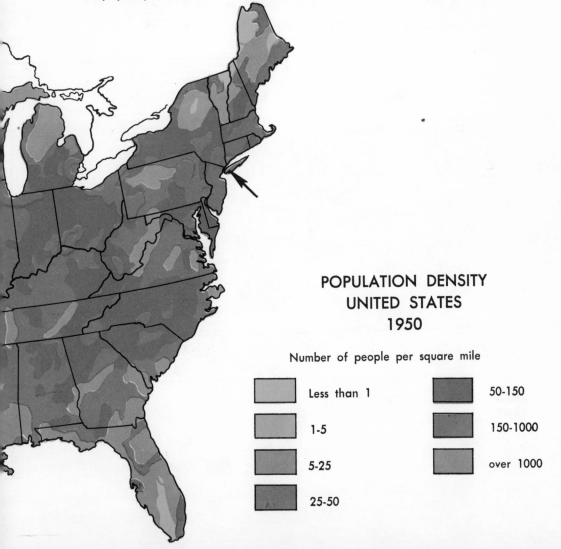

POPULATION DENSITY
UNITED STATES
1950

Number of people per square mile

Less than 1		50-150
1-5		150-1000
5-25		over 1000
25-50		

Do maps help our study of the past?

Maps have pictured for us interesting facts about our country. They have shown us how these facts are related.

The study of maps can help us in another way. It can show us the events of the past which help explain the present.

Of course we need books to study the past. But we need maps, too. They make the events that happened long ago easier to understand.

Our country has grown rapidly since the first settlers came to the Atlantic shore. This map shows us how and when new areas were added to the United States during the first hundred years of its growth.

HOW THE UNITED STATES GREW

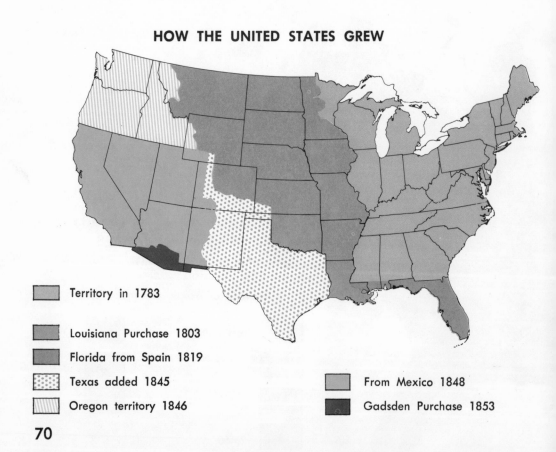

Territory in 1783

Louisiana Purchase 1803

Florida from Spain 1819

Texas added 1845

Oregon territory 1846

From Mexico 1848

Gadsden Purchase 1853

Summary

Knowing how to use maps and globes makes the study of our world more interesting. Skill with maps is useful for travelers of all kinds.

A globe is the truest picture of the earth, because it has the same shape. On all maps, the true picture of the earth is changed in some way, because maps are flat.

Maps are used to show most kinds of information that we need to know about the earth. Maps are easier to handle and can be printed in books. They can show either large or small areas of the earth. If you want to know facts about a certain country, you look for maps to show you these facts.

Here are some examples of the kinds of information about a country which you can find on maps:

You can tell whether it has a seacoast, and what the shape of the coastline is. You can find the mountains and lowlands.

By using lines of longitude and latitude, you can find its important cities. You can find distances between cities by using the map scale.

You can find out how much rain falls each year on different parts of the country. You can see which crops are raised, and where.

You can learn the best routes to travel between principal cities, by road and by air.

These are just a few of the facts you can learn about a country through map study. It is one of the most fascinating ways to learn about the world.

Concept Index

Shown below in bold type are those words which are underlined and defined in the text. The first number appearing after each of these words is the number of the page on which it is defined. Other important concepts are listed in lighter type. Pronunciation is given for all words which might be difficult to pronounce.

acreage (ā'kĕr ĭj) 66
Antarctic 11
Arctic 11

boundaries (boun'dá rĭz) 49

climate (klī'mĭt) 60-61
color 46-49
continent (kŏn'tĭ nĕnt) 12, 49
contour (kŏn'tŏŏr) **lines** 54-55

degree (dĕ grē') 14-15
direction (dĭ rĕk'shŭn) 25-29
distance (dĭs'tăns) 30, 32-34

elevation (ĕl'ĕ vā'shŭn) 48
equal area map 44
equator (ĕ kwā'tĕr) 10

forests 65

globe 7-18
Greenwich (grĕn'ĭch) **England** 14

hemisphere (hĕm'ĭ sfēr) 11-12

interrupted (ĭn tĕr rŭp'tĕd)
projection (prŏ jĕk'shŭn) 42, 43
isotherm (ī'sŏ thûrm) 61

land use 66-67
latitude (lăt'ĭ tūd) 13, 15-16
legend (lĕj'ĕnd) 51-52
longitude (lŏn'jĭ tūd) 13-14, 16

magnetic (măg nĕt'ĭk) **north** 27
map 19-71
map compass 26
map scale 30-33
meridian (mĕ rĭd'ĭ ăn) 14
Mercator's (mûr kā'tĕrz)
projection (prŏ jĕk'shŭn) 40-41, 43
metropolitan (mĕt rŏ pŏl'ĭ tăn)
area 69
mileage table 34-35

North Pole 10

occluded (ŏ klōōd'ĕd) **front** 62, 63

parallel (păr'ă lĕl) 15
physical (fĭz'ĭ kăl) **map** 57, 63
population (pŏp'ŭ lā'shŭn) 68
position (pŏ zĭsh'ŭn) 13
precipitation (prĕ sĭp'ĭ tā'shŭn) 60
projection (prŏ jĕk'shŭn) 39

rainfall 60

sea level 48
South Pole 10
sphere (sfēr) 11
stationary (stā'shŭn ĕr'ĭ) **front** 62, 63
symbol (sĭm'băl) 50-53

tropical (trŏp'ĭ kăl) **region** 11

vertical (vûr'tĭ kăl) **obstruction**
(ŏb strŭk'shŭn) 58

weather map 62-63

72